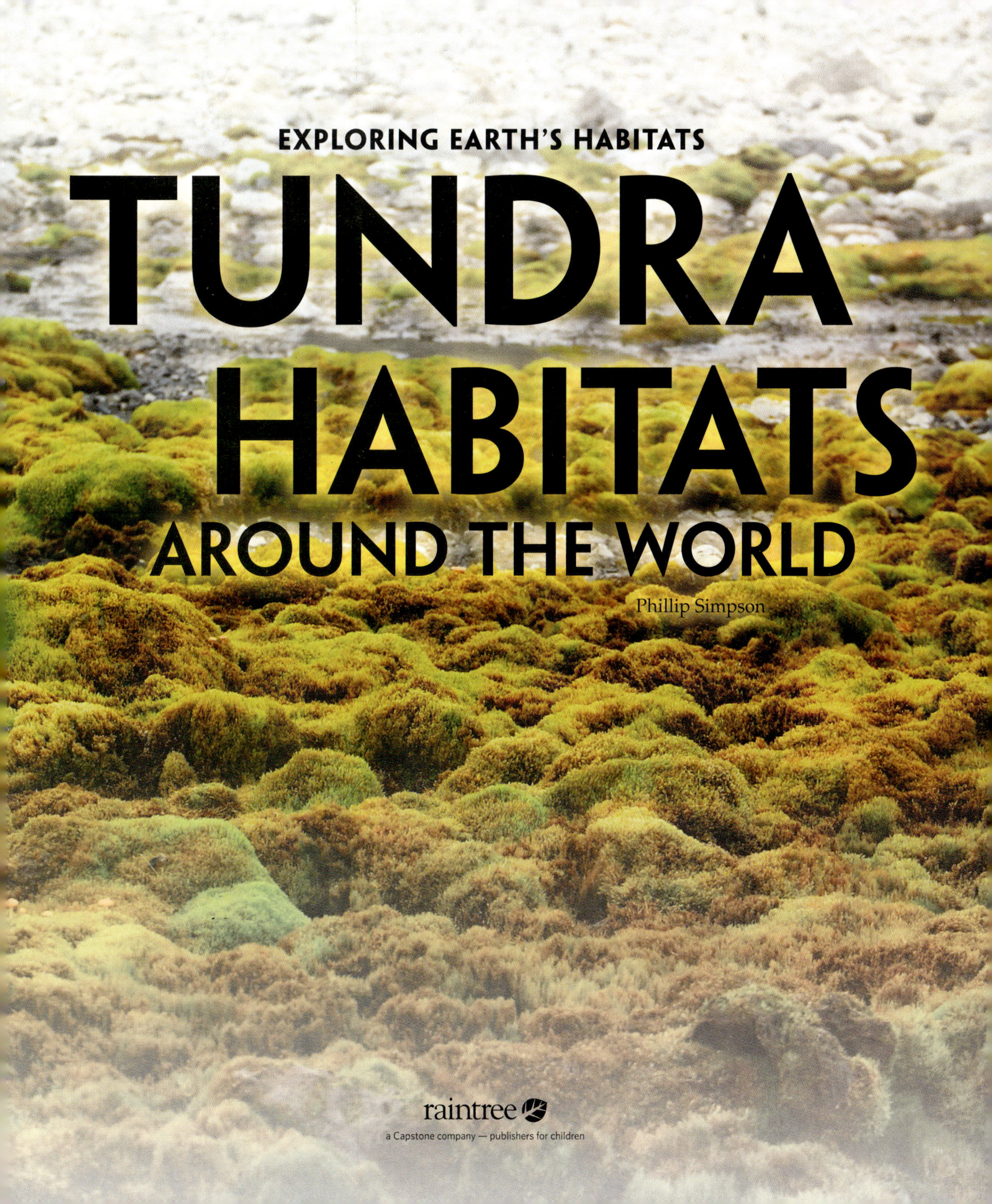

EXPLORING EARTH'S HABITATS

TUNDRA HABITATS AROUND THE WORLD

Phillip Simpson

raintree
a Capstone company — publishers for children

Raintree is an imprint of Capstone Global Library Limited, a company incorporated in England and Wales having its registered office at 264 Banbury Road, Oxford, OX2 7DY – Registered company number: 6695582

www.raintree.co.uk
myorders@raintree.co.uk

Edited by Gina Kammer
Designed by Julie Peters
Original illustrations © Capstone Global Library Limited 2020
Picture research by Morgan Walters
Production by Kathy McColley
Originated by Capstone Global Library Ltd
Printed and bound in India

ISBN: 978 1 4747 8584 6 (hardback)
ISBN: 978 1 4747 8590 7 (paperback)

British Library Cataloguing in Publication Data
A full catalogue record for this book is available from the British Library.

Acknowledgements
Alamy: Megapress, 25, P.A. Lawrence, LLC., 24, Renato Granieri, 9; iStockphoto: aaprophoto, 16, RelaxedPace, 17; Newscom: Eric Baccega/agefotostock, 18, SABRINA BLANCHARD, JONATHAN WALTER, JONATHAN STOREY AFP, 27, SOPHIE RAMIS, ALAIN BOMMENEL AFP, 28, Ton Koene/agefotostock/, 19; Science Source: Gary Hincks, bottom 8; Shutterstock: Andy Fogelsonger, spread 18, spread 20-21, David Dennis, bottom left 4, 12, Denis Burdin, spread 26-27, spread 28-29, Designua, top 5, evgenii mitroshin, 20, Galyna Andrushko, 11, Gregory A. Pozhvanov, (tundra) Cover, bottom left 10, Grezova Olga, 13, indukas, 15, Natalia Davidovich, (moss) design element throughout, nenets, spread 22-23, spread 24-25, nubephoto, (man) Cover, Peter Hermes Furian, bottom left 6, Tatiana Gasich, 21, Troutnut, spread 10-11, spread 12-13, spread 14-15, spread 16-17, ugljesa, bottom 7, Vladimir Melnik, spread 4-5, spread 6-7, spread 8-9, Vladimir Melnikov, 23, Volodymyr Burdiak, 14

CONTENTS

CHAPTER 1

FROZEN GROUND

Before you is a bare wasteland, frozen and hard. Not a single tree is in sight. The freezing wind threatens to blow you over. It chills you to the bone. Where are you? You're in the tundra.

Tundras are one of the five main habitats. These large areas have certain types of climates, plants and animals. The five main habitats are aquatic, forest, desert, grassland and tundra. Tundras are the coldest habitats on Earth and are mostly treeless. The tundra habitat covers almost 10 per cent of Earth's surface.

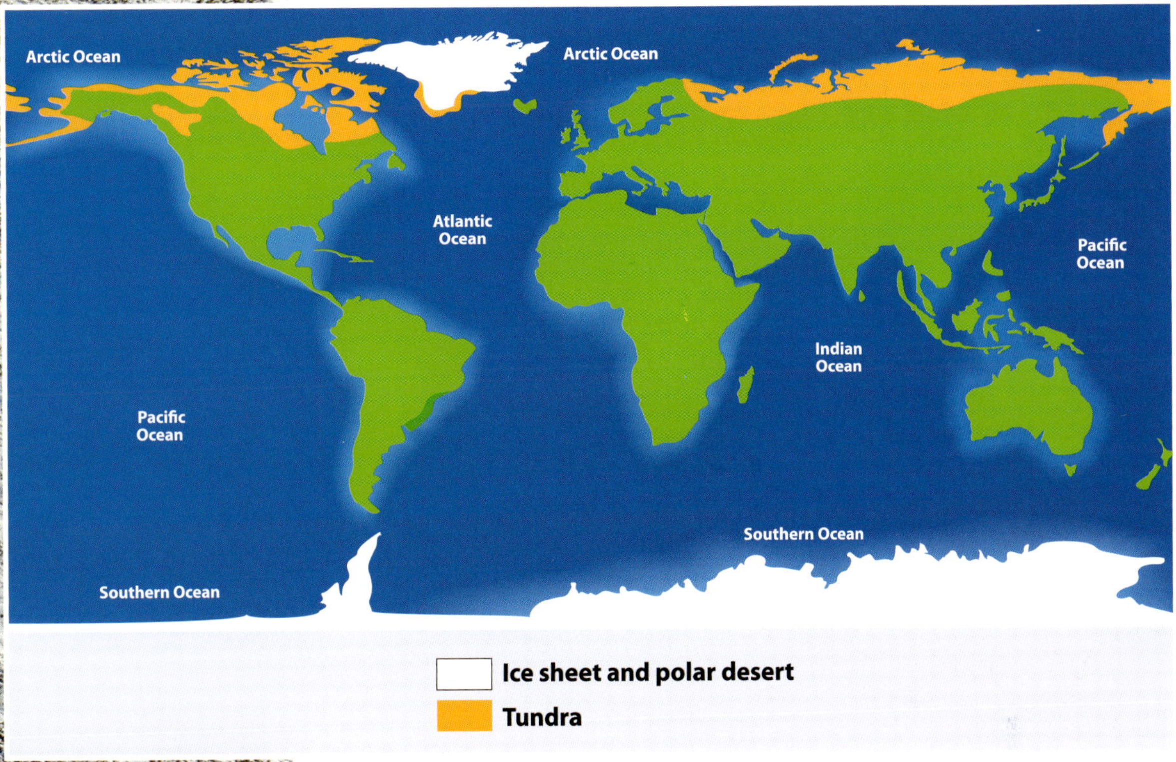

The tundra habitat features large areas of bare ground and rock. Short plants such as mosses, **lichens** and small scrub cover the ground. Few humans or animals live in this habitat because of the cold and lack of food. However, the few plants and animals living in tundras have **adapted** to the unique conditions and couldn't survive elsewhere. The three types of tundras are Arctic tundra, Antarctic tundra and alpine tundra.

adapt change in order to survive; a change in an animal or plant to better fit its environment is called an adaptation
lichen flat, moss-like plant; it is made up of a kind of algae and a fungus that grow together

ARCTIC TUNDRA

The Arctic tundra is found in the Arctic Circle and the areas surrounding the North Pole. The Arctic tundra covers parts of northern Europe, Asia and North America. These regions are very cold. The Arctic tundra has average temperatures as low as minus 34 degrees Celsius in the winter months. In summer, the temperature in the Arctic tundra rises only to about 10°C. The Arctic subsoil – the area directly beneath the topsoil – is always frozen. This soil layer is called **permafrost**. It also contains frozen water.

WINTER SOLSTICE

21 or 22 December

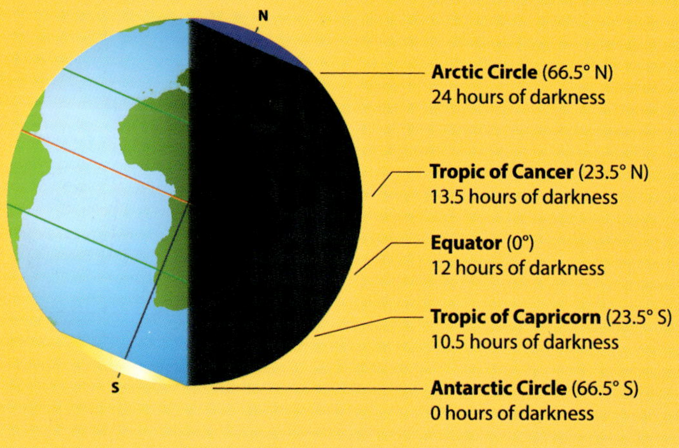

FACT

The winter solstice in the northern hemisphere is the moment when the sun is furthest from the north pole. However, people often recognize the winter solstice as the full 24-hour day.

ANTARCTIC TUNDRA

The Antarctic tundra covers the smallest area of land. It's found on the continent of Antarctica as well as several nearby islands including South Georgia and South Sandwich islands. On the Antarctic Peninsula, only small areas of rocky soil support tundra and permafrost. The rest of Antarctica is mainly covered by ice fields. It's too dry and cold for plant life. Average annual temperatures in the Antarctic are –49°C.

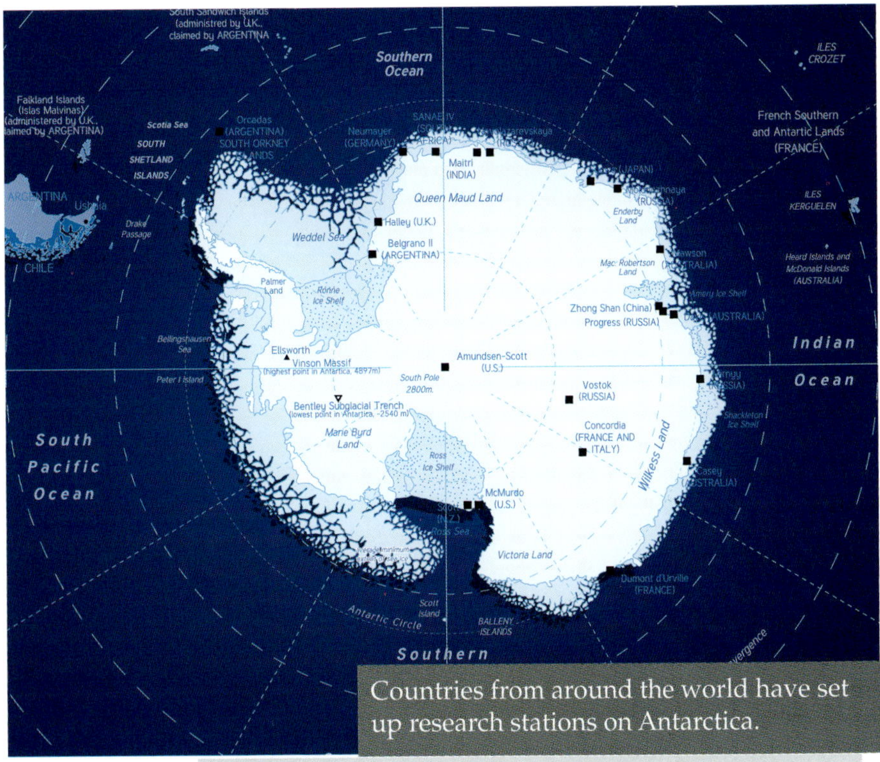

Countries from around the world have set up research stations on Antarctica.

permafrost layer of soil, usually below the topsoil, permanently frozen during both winter and summer

ALPINE TUNDRA

Alpine tundra is found above the **treeline** on high mountains all around the world. The climate is too cold and windy at these levels for trees to grow. Alpine tundra only extends to the snow line, which is always covered in snow – even in summer. However, compared to the other types of tundras, the alpine tundra has a longer growing season. Temperatures range up to about 10°C in summer to well below freezing in winter. Alpine tundra usually has no permafrost.

The alpine tundra starts at about 3,100 metres.

FACT
The word tundra comes from people from Finland, who called their cold treeless areas "tunturia", meaning treeless plain.

treeline point on mountainsides beyond which trees do not grow

CHAPTER 2

HARDY PLANTS AND ANIMALS

Tundra plants and animals are hardy. They have to be! The frozen ground, cold weather and windy landscape require unique features for survival. But tundra plants and animals are up to the challenge.

FACT
The Arctic tundra has about 1,700 types of plants. Most are small and are sometimes called "ground cover" because they cover the ground.

TUNDRA PLANT LIFE

Antarctic and Arctic plant life are similar, with many types of lichens, grasses, liverworts and mosses. Plants are unable to push roots deep into the frozen ground. For that reason, it's difficult for large plants such as trees to survive. Tundra plants have adapted to the high winds and the frozen soil. They are small and grow low to the ground. They group together and spread their roots over a wide area. Some plants in the Arctic tundra grow under a layer of snow.

The most common type of grass in the Arctic tundra is cotton grass.

Plants in the alpine tundra are similar to those in the Arctic tundra. They have almost identical **environmental** conditions. Similar to the Arctic tundra, shrubs, mosses and lichens are plentiful. Alpine tundra grasses include tough tussock grass. This grass survives by quickly growing long roots.

Plants found in Greenland's tundra include grasses, bearberry, red algae and mosses.

environmental relating to the natural world and the impact of human activity on its condition

Caribou moss

A common alpine tundra plant is the caribou moss, which is actually a type of lichen. Caribou moss can survive for a long time without water. It dries out and then starts to grow again when there is water.

Many flowering plants have thick hairs on their stems and leaves. The hairs protect them from harsh winds. Some plants have adapted by taking longer to form flower buds. They survive the winter below the soil's surface. They then emerge during the few weeks of summer to open and spread their seeds.

TUNDRA ANIMAL LIFE

Animals in the tundra have adapted to its extreme temperatures and tolerate long, cold winters. Their young are born and grow up in summer to avoid the harsh winter. Some **hibernate** in winter when food is scarce.

The brown bear is one of the few mammals that live in the Arctic tundra all year long. During summer, it stores up food as a layer of fat underneath its skin. The fat keeps the bear warm and is converted into energy. The energy keeps the bear alive in winter when it goes into the deep sleep of hibernation.

Brown bear

Musk ox

The musk ox also lives in the Arctic tundra for the whole year. Its coat has a short layer and a long layer of fur. Air trapped between these fur layers is warmed by body heat. The trapped air acts as **insulation** from the cold. The long fur protects the animal from wind and water. The musk ox's large, hard hooves allow it to break ice and drink the water below during winter.

hibernate to go into a resting state over the winter, as if in a deep sleep
insulation material that stops heat, sound or cold from entering or escaping

A number of **herbivores** survive in the Arctic tundra because of its plant life. Most tundra birds and mammals don't live there year-round. They use the tundra as a summer home. Many birds eat the plants that grow in summer. They then leave for warmer climates in winter.

Unlike the Arctic tundra, the Antarctic tundra doesn't have many animal species, as the tundra areas are so small. The animals that do make their homes there include seals, penguins, hares and albatross.

Albatross near Antarctica

Caribou

Animals in the alpine tundra include mammals such as caribou. The caribou have adapted to this region by being able to survive on lichen. They have **microorganisms** in their stomachs that let them eat lichen. Very few other animals eat lichen. Scientists think that the caribou have evolved to eat lichen when other animals couldn't.

herbivore animal that eats only plants
microorganism living thing too small to be seen without a microscope

CHAPTER 3

HUMAN SURVIVORS

Tundra habitats are cold, harsh and remote regions. Would you want to live in such a region? Some people do! Few people have settled in these places, compared to other habitats. However, evidence suggests that humans have lived in tundra regions for more than 20,000 years.

A teenage Nenet girl stands by her tent in Yamal, Russia.

A young Inuit boy lives in Gjoa Haven, Canada. Inuits hunt animals including polar bears, fish and Arctic hares.

Early humans may have been forced into the tundra from milder areas by other humans. Perhaps they moved into the tundra areas because there weren't as many people. This meant less **competition** for food and water. Many of these people were **nomadic**, following herds of animals. Today, many people in tundra areas, such as those in Alaska, live in permanent villages and towns. They deal with the same things most other people do in winter, including problems such as frozen pipes!

The largest human group in the tundra is the Inuit people. They live in the Arctic tundra in places such as Canada and Greenland. The Inuit live near the coast where they hunt caribou, seal, fish and even the occasional whale. They make **traditional** clothing out of caribou skins and fur, just as their ancestors did.

competition situation in which two or more people are trying to get the same thing
nomadic travelling from place to place in search of food and water
traditional relating to customs that are handed down

The Innu are First Nations people who live in the tundra areas of northern Labrador and Quebec in Canada. The tundra environment once provided all they needed to survive. They hunted caribou for food and to make clothing and tools. Because of overhunting by other settlers, the numbers of caribou shrank over time. This led to the starvation of many of the Innu people. Many who survived were forced to move out of these areas.

A young boy dresses in thick, warm clothing in the Arctic tundra.

FACT

Tundra regions are also popular with tourists. The combination of wildlife, amazing scenery and few humans make tundras great for hunting, hiking, camping and wildlife watching.

The Yakut live in the tundra in the Russian region of Siberia. Fishing is an important part of the Yakut economy. They eat some of the fish and sell the rest. They hunt animals for their fur, which they use for clothing and to sell. The Yakut also breed hardy horses and cattle. The Yakut are nomadic and move twice a year – during summer to store hay and in winter for shelter.

A group of young Yakuts dress in traditional clothing and hold plates of foods in Yakutsk, Russia.

People travel to tundras for their natural resources, even though they are remote and hard to reach. Oil, natural gas, petroleum and uranium are mined in these regions.

First Nations any of the indigenous peoples or native communities of Canada, especially one formally recognized by the Canadian government

CHAPTER 4

THE HUMAN THREAT

The tundra habitat is a valued and important **ecosystem**. This habitat gives tourists the opportunity to see unique plants and animals or enjoy winter sports such as skiing. People also mine valuable oil and resources. However, people have greatly impacted the tundra wilderness by building homes, ski resorts, mines and roads. Hunting has affected animal life. In addition, searching and drilling for oil has polluted the environment and threatened wildlife. Other threats include erosion and pesticides used to control insects.

Tundra doesn't grow back quickly if disturbed. For example, vehicles damage the tundra and the plants on its surface. The vehicle tracks remain for decades.

The hunt for **fossil fuels** is particularly damaging in the Arctic tundra. It's difficult to build pipelines through the permafrost. Large areas of tundra in the paths of pipelines are destroyed. In addition, oil or gas pipelines can break. The spilled fuel can kill wildlife and damage the ecosystem.

An oil field in western Siberia

ecosystem system of living and non-living things in an environment

fossil fuels fuels such as oil, coal and natural gas made from decayed plants and animals that have been converted by heat and pressure in Earth's crust over hundreds of millions of years

Global warming is the greatest threat to tundra habitats. Humans continue to release **greenhouse gases** into the atmosphere. These gases are contributing to the heating of the planet. They create a barrier in Earth's atmosphere that keeps heat from escaping.

Global warming has already changed the tundra ecosystems. Temperatures have risen. With the rising temperatures, tundra fires have increased. Dead plants and peat, a type of decayed plant material, are extremely **flammable**.

A fire burning in the Alaska tundra

flammable can easily catch fire
global warming increase in the average temperature of Earth's climate
greenhouse gas gas in a planet's atmosphere that traps heat energy from the sun; most greenhouse gases are water vapour, carbon dioxide, methane, nitrous oxide and ozone

A forest destroyed by a fire in James Bay, Quebec, Canada

These fires reduce ground cover such as lichens, which the caribou need to survive. Fewer lichens and other plants will eventually have an impact on animal life. With no food, tundra animals will become threatened and perhaps face extinction.

FACT

Fires are not uncommon in the tundra. Lightning from a storm caused nearly 14 hectares of land to burn in 2018 in Alaska.

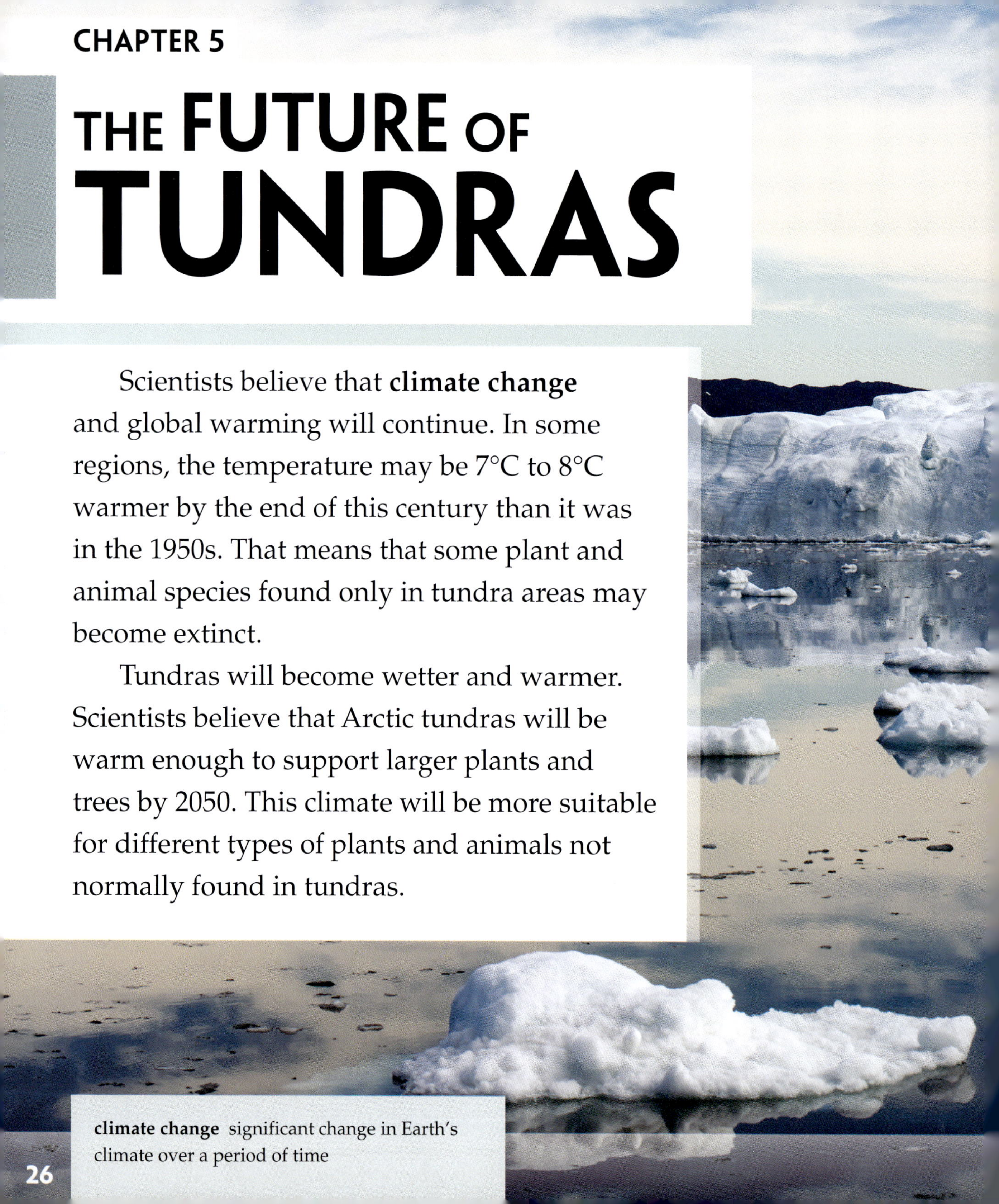

CHAPTER 5

THE FUTURE OF TUNDRAS

Scientists believe that **climate change** and global warming will continue. In some regions, the temperature may be 7°C to 8°C warmer by the end of this century than it was in the 1950s. That means that some plant and animal species found only in tundra areas may become extinct.

Tundras will become wetter and warmer. Scientists believe that Arctic tundras will be warm enough to support larger plants and trees by 2050. This climate will be more suitable for different types of plants and animals not normally found in tundras.

climate change significant change in Earth's climate over a period of time

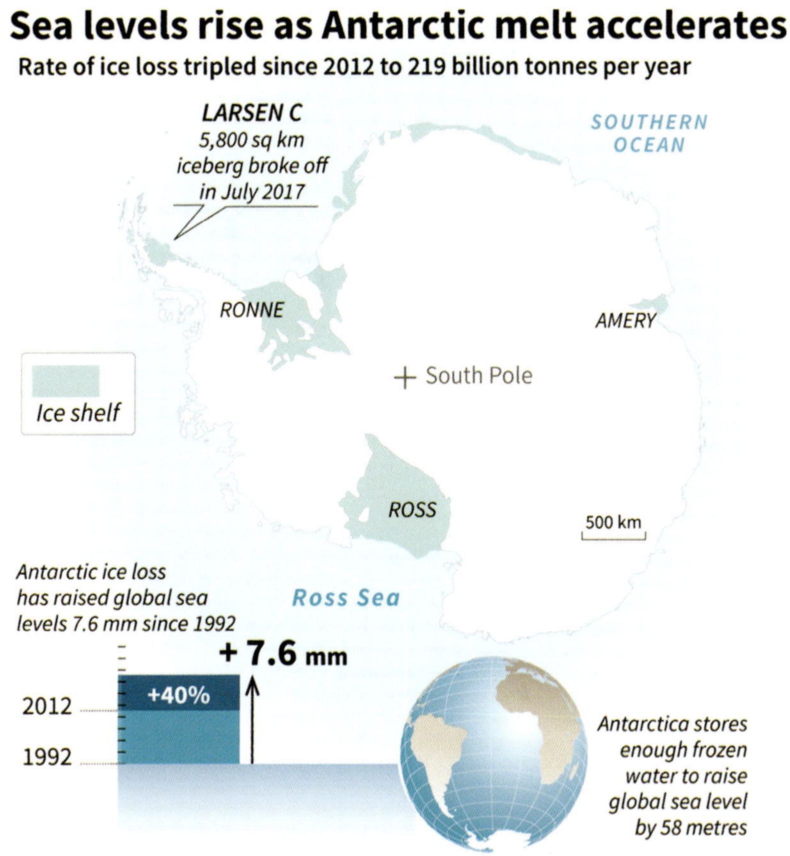

As temperatures rise, polar ice melts and sea levels rise.

While this may sound good for other species, it isn't so good for native plants and animals in tundra regions. They will face extinction. It's estimated that the tundra will decrease by 33 to 44 per cent by the end of this century. One study shows that as much as 77 per cent of the tundra will have disappeared by 2100.

The fate of permafrost is also a future concern. Tundra habitats store large amounts of dead organic matter, or carbon, in the frozen soil. Some of this matter has been frozen for thousands of years. Rising temperatures will thaw the permafrost. The organic material will begin to decay. As it does, it will release carbon dioxide into the atmosphere in the form of greenhouse gases.

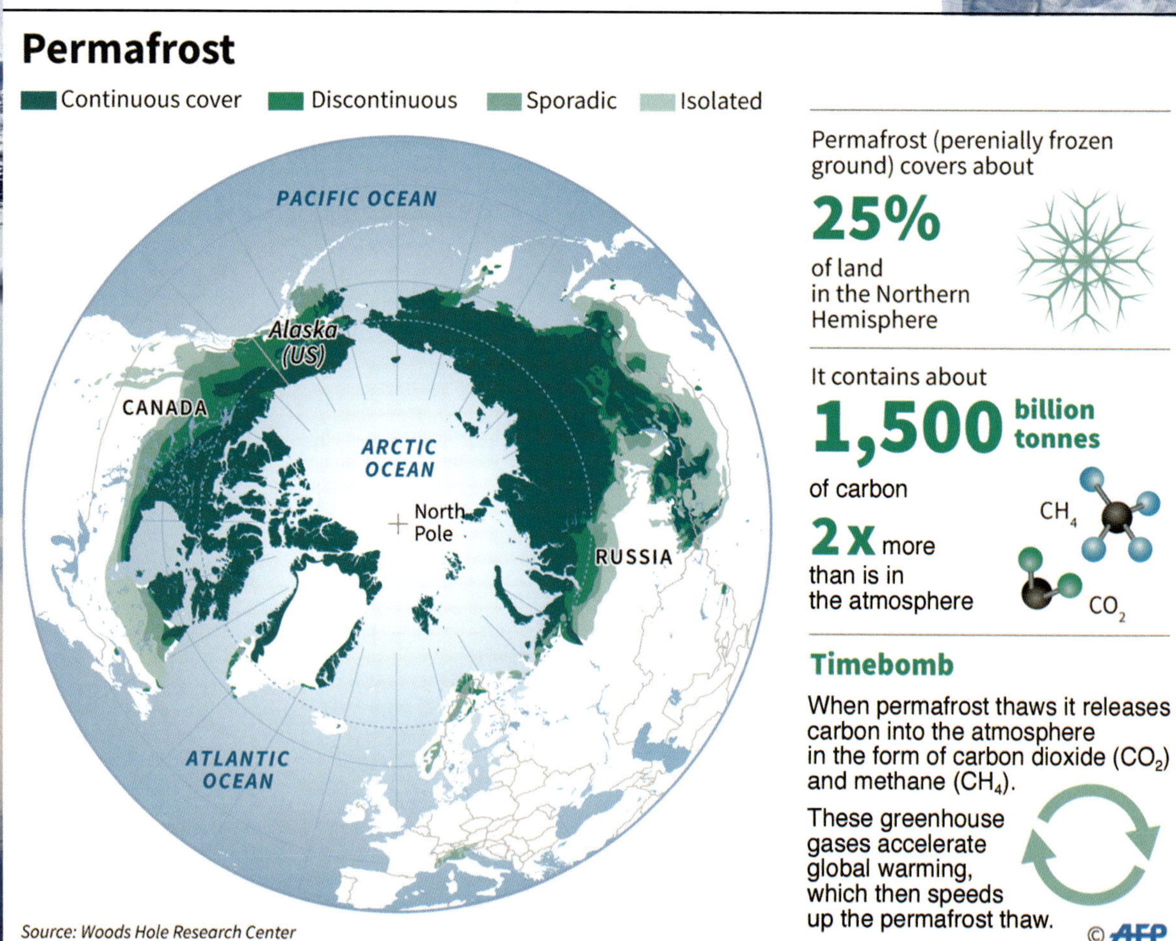

FACT

What can you do to help? Less demand for fossil fuels will help preserve the tundra. Use solar energy in your home. Ask adults about installing solar panels. Do simple things to save energy such as turning off lights when you leave a room.

Greenhouse gases speed the thawing and add to global warming. If global warming continues as scientists believe it will, these habitats face destruction. The wildlife could become extinct. People living in the tundra will face problems as well. Melting permafrost causes roads and houses to sink. Pipelines could buckle and break.

However, reducing greenhouse gases can help protect Earth's tundra habitats. People can switch to energy such as solar and wind. Creating reserves and protected tundra areas to reduce human impact can also help. Conservation efforts can limit construction of roads, mines and pipelines. It's up to everyone to work together to preserve this unique habitat.

GLOSSARY

adapt change in order to survive; a change in an animal or plant to better fit its environment is called an adaptation

climate change significant change in Earth's climate over a period of time

competition situation in which two or more people are trying to get the same thing

ecosystem system of living and non-living things in an environment

environmental relating to the natural world and the impact of human activity on its condition

First Nations any of the indigenous peoples or native communities of Canada, especially one formally recognized by the Canadian government

flammable can easily catch fire

fossil fuels fuels such as oil, coal and natural gas made from decayed plants and animals that have been converted by heat and pressure in Earth's crust over hundreds of millions of years

global warming increase in the average temperature of Earth's climate

greenhouse gas gas in a planet's atmosphere that traps heat energy from the sun; most greenhouse gases are water vapour, carbon dioxide, methane, nitrous oxide and ozone

herbivore animal that eats only plants

hibernate go into a resting state over the winter, as if in a deep sleep

insulation material that stops heat, sound or cold from entering or escaping

lichen flat, moss-like plant; it is made up of a kind of algae and a fungus that grow together

microorganism living thing too small to be seen without a microscope

nomadic travelling from place to place in search of food and water

permafrost layer of soil, usually below topsoil, permanently frozen during both winter and summer

traditional relating to customs that are handed down

treeline point on mountainsides beyond which trees do not grow

FIND OUT MORE

BOOKS

All About Earth (Discover Earth Science), Sara L. Latta (Raintree, 2017)

Arctic Tundra (Earth's Last Frontiers), Ellen Labrecque (Raintree, 2016)

Humans Environmental Impact (Humans and Our Planet), Ava Sawyer (Raintree, 2018)

WEBSITES

bbc.co.uk/bitesize/topics/zbnnb69q/articles/zcgbjty
Take the tundra food chain challenge and find out more about food chains and habitats in a tundra habitat.

dkfindout.com/uk/history/native-americans/inuit
Learn more about how the Inuit made their home in the Arctic tundra, including a tour of an igloo.

COMPREHENSION QUESTIONS

1. What are the pros and cons of human influence in the tundra? Do you think humans are justified in exploring and utilizing the resources in the tundra? Use evidence to explain your thinking.
2. Why is the permafrost so important? What will happen if the permafrost melts?
3. Name the ways plants and animals have adapted to extreme environments such as the tundra. Why is it necessary for plants and animals to adapt to an environment?

INDEX